MW01516125

Patrick Mahomes

The Boy Who Fell in Love with

Football and Never Gave Up.

Benjamin Danielson

This book belongs to...........................

....

COPYRIGHT © 2024 by Benjamin Danielson

All rights reserved. No part of this publication may be reproduced, distributed, or transmitted in any form or by any means, including photocopying, recording, or other electronic or mechanical methods, without the prior written permission of the publisher, except in the case of brief quotations embodied in critical reviews and certain other noncommercial uses permitted by copyright law.

Trademarks and pictures are used without permission. Use of the trademark is not authorized by, associated with, or sponsored by the trademark owners. All trademarks and pictures used within this book are used with no intent to infringe on the trademark owners and only used for clarifying purposes.

TABLE OF CONTENTS

INTRODUCTION

Have you ever dreamed of becoming a famous athlete? Maybe you've imagined yourself scoring the winning touchdown in a big game or hitting a home run in front of a cheering crowd. Well, Patrick Mahomes lived that dream. He's a football superstar who plays for the Kansas City Chiefs in the NFL.

But before he became a football hero, Patrick loved playing baseball. He spent hours practicing his swing and trying to hit his dad's fastballs. But as he grew older, Patrick realized that football was his true passion. He loved the excitement of the game, the strategy, and the teamwork.

In this book, you'll learn about Patrick's journey from a young boy who loved baseball to a world-class football player. You'll discover how he overcame challenges, faced setbacks, and never gave up on his dreams. Get ready to be inspired by the incredible story of Patrick Mahomes, The Boy Who Fell in Love with Football and Never Gave Up.

CHAPTER 1:

A STAR IS BORN

➤ **Growing up in Texas**

Patrick Mahomes grew up in a small town in Texas called Whitehouse. It was a place where everyone knew everyone, and the kids loved to play outside. Patrick was no different. He spent his days riding bikes, playing baseball, and dreaming of becoming a big-time athlete.

Patrick's dad, Pat, was a former Major League Baseball pitcher. He taught Patrick everything he knew about the game, from how to throw a fastball to how to slide into second base. Patrick loved baseball, but he also had a secret passion: football.

"I remember playing football in the backyard with my friends,"

Patrick said. **"We'd make up our own rules and have the craziest games. It was so much fun."**

Patrick's mom, Randi, supported him in all his endeavors. She would drive him to baseball practice, football games, and even his piano lessons. She was always there to cheer him on and give him a hug when he needed it.

Early love for baseball

Patrick's love for baseball began at a very young age. He would spend hours in the backyard, practicing his swing and trying to hit his dad's fastballs. His dad would pitch to him until the sun went down, and Patrick would never get tired.

"I remember one time I hit a home run over the fence," Patrick said with a smile. **"My dad**

was so proud. He told me I was going to be a big star someday."

Patrick's mom would often take him to watch the Texas Rangers play at the ballpark. He loved the smell of hot dogs and popcorn, the sound of the crowd cheering, and the excitement of watching his favorite players. Patrick dreamed of one day playing in the big leagues and making his family proud.

Discovering football

Patrick's love for baseball was strong, but he also had a growing passion for football. He started playing tackle football when he was in elementary school, and he quickly discovered that he had a natural talent for the game.

"I remember my first football game," Patrick said. "I was so nervous, but as soon as I stepped onto the field, I felt right at home. I knew I was going to love this sport."

Patrick played quarterback, and he was a natural leader on the field. He had a strong arm, a quick mind, and a knack for making big plays. His teammates loved playing with him, and his coaches were amazed by his talent.

"Patrick was a special player from the very beginning," said his high school football coach. "He had a unique ability to make everyone around him better. He was a true leader."

CHAPTER 2:

THE QUARTERBACK KID

➤High school football stardom

Patrick's high school football career
was a whirlwind of success. He led
his team to multiple state
championships, and he was named
the state's Player of the Year. His
amazing performances caught the
attention of college scouts, and he

received offers from some of the top universities in the country.

"It was a crazy time," Patrick said. **"I was getting calls from coaches all over the place. It was a lot to take in, but I was excited about the opportunity to play college football."**

Patrick's senior year was especially memorable. He threw for over 5,000 yards and scored 50 touchdowns. He was named a first-team All-American and was invited to play in the prestigious Under Armour All-America Game.

"I'll never forget that game," Patrick said. "It was a dream come true to play with some of the best high school players in the country."

Committing to Texas Tech

Patrick's decision to commit to Texas Tech University was a big one. He had offers from many other schools, but he felt a strong connection to the Red Raiders. He loved the coaching staff, the campus, and the city of Lubbock.

"I knew Texas Tech was the right place for me," Patrick said. "I felt like I could really thrive there, both on and off the field."

Patrick's commitment to Texas Tech was met with excitement and anticipation from fans and the coaching staff. They knew they were getting a special player who had the potential to be a star.

"We were thrilled to have Patrick join our program," said Texas Tech head coach Kliff Kingsbury. "He's a once-in-a-generation talent. We knew he could be a special player for us."

Freshman season challenges

Patrick's freshman season at Texas Tech was a bit of a rollercoaster. He saw limited playing time early in the year, but he eventually worked his way into the starting lineup.

"It was tough to sit on the bench," Patrick said. **"I wanted to be out there helping the team win. But I**

knew I had to be patient and wait for my opportunity."

When Patrick finally got his chance to start, he made the most of it. He threw for over 2,000 yards and 15 touchdowns. He also rushed for 250 yards and scored 5 touchdowns.

"Patrick's freshman season was a big step in the right direction," said Kingsbury. "He showed us that he was ready to be a starting

quarterback at the college level."

CHAPTER 3:

RISING TO THE

CHALLENGE

➢ Sophomore breakout season

Patrick's sophomore season at Texas Tech was a breakout year. He started every game and led the Red Raiders to a bowl game. He threw for over 5,000 yards and 53 touchdowns, and he was named the Big 12 Offensive Player of the Year.

"It was a dream come true," Patrick said. "I never thought I would be able to put up numbers like that. It was a special season."

One of the highlights of Patrick's sophomore year was his game against Oklahoma. He threw for 582 yards and 8 touchdowns, leading the Red Raiders to a thrilling victory.

"That was one of the best games I've ever played," Patrick said. "The atmosphere was electric. The crowd was going crazy. It was an unforgettable experience."

Patrick's performance in his sophomore season helped establish him as one of the top quarterbacks in college football. He was a Heisman Trophy finalist, and he was named a first-team All-American.

Setting Records

Patrick's sophomore season was filled with record-breaking performances. He broke the Big 12 single-season passing yards record, the Big 12 single-season touchdown passes record, and the Texas Tech single-season passing yards record.

"It was surreal," Patrick said. "I was just trying to play my best and help

the team win. To break records was a bonus."

One of Patrick's most impressive performances came against Kansas State. He threw for 598 yards and 6 touchdowns, leading the Red Raiders to a come-from-behind victory.

"That game was a classic," Patrick said. "We were down by a lot, but we never gave up. We kept fighting, and we were able to pull it out in the end."

Patrick's record-breaking performances helped cement his status as one of the greatest quarterbacks in college football history. He was a Heisman Trophy finalist, and he was named a first-team All-American.

Heisman Trophy contender

Patrick's sophomore season was a Heisman Trophy-worthy performance. He was a finalist for the award, and he finished second in the voting. While he didn't win the trophy, Patrick was still incredibly proud of his accomplishments.

"It was an honor to be a Heisman finalist," Patrick said. "To be mentioned among the best players in the country was a dream come true."

Patrick's Heisman Trophy candidacy helped him gain national attention. He was featured on SportsCenter, ESPN, and other major sports networks. He was also invited to appear on the Late Show with Stephen Colbert.

"It was a crazy experience," Patrick said. "I never thought I would be on national television. It was a lot of fun, but it was also a lot of work."

CHAPTER 4:

THE NFL DRAFT

<u>First overall pick by the Kansas City Chiefs</u>

Patrick's college career was nothing short of spectacular. He was a two-time Big 12 Offensive Player of the Year, a Heisman Trophy finalist, and a first-team All-American. His incredible talent and potential made him a highly sought-after prospect for the NFL Draft.

The 2017 NFL Draft was a momentous occasion for Patrick. He knew he was going to be a high draft pick, but he never expected to be selected with the first overall pick.

"It was a dream come true," Patrick said. "To be picked first overall by the Kansas City Chiefs was an incredible honor."

The Chiefs were thrilled to have Patrick join their team. They believed he was the future of their franchise, and they were excited to see what he could do in the NFL.

"Patrick is a generational talent," said Chiefs general manager John Dorsey. **"He's the kind of player who can change a franchise. We're so excited to have him in Kansas City."**

Rookie season excitement

Patrick's rookie season with the Kansas City Chiefs was a whirlwind of excitement. He was immediately named the starting quarterback, and he was eager to prove himself at the highest level of professional football.

"I was so excited to be playing in the NFL," Patrick said. "It was a dream come true. I knew I had to work hard and play my best to make the most of this opportunity."

Patrick's rookie season was a mixed bag. He showed flashes of brilliance, but he also struggled at times. He finished the season with a record of 5-11, but he showed enough promise to make the Chiefs believe that he was the future of their franchise.

"Patrick had a good rookie season," said Chiefs head coach Andy Reid. "He's a talented player, and he's only going to get better. I'm excited to see what he can do in the future."

Patrick's rookie season was a valuable learning experience. He learned how to adjust to the speed and physicality of the NFL game. He also learned the importance of preparation and hard work.

Proving himself on the big stage

Patrick's second season in the NFL was a breakout year. He started all 16 games and led the Chiefs to the playoffs for the first time in five years. He threw for over 5,000 yards and 50 touchdowns, and he was named the NFL Offensive Player of the Year.

"It was a special season," Patrick said. "I felt like I really came into my own as a quarterback. I was able to make all the throws, and I was able to lead the team to victory."

One of Patrick's most impressive performances came against the Denver Broncos. He threw for 509 yards and 6 touchdowns, leading the Chiefs to a come-from-behind victory.

"That was one of the best games I've ever played," Patrick said. **"I was in the zone. I was feeling it. Everything I threw went right."**

Patrick's second season proved that he was one of the best quarterbacks in the NFL. He was a Pro Bowl selection, and he was named the NFL MVP.

CHAPTER 5:

THE COMEBACK KID

➤ *Overcoming injuries*

Patrick's career has not been without its challenges. In 2019, he suffered a serious ankle injury that threatened to end his season. But Patrick was determined to come back stronger than ever.

"It was tough," Patrick said. "I was in a lot of pain, and I wasn't sure if I would be able to play again. But I never gave up. I worked hard every day to get back to 100%."

With the help of his doctors, trainers, and teammates, Patrick made a full recovery from his injury. He returned to the field in Week 10 and led the Chiefs to a playoff berth.

"It was a miracle," Patrick said. "I never thought I would be able to come back and play at this level. But I did it. I proved to myself that I could overcome anything."

Patrick's comeback from injury was a testament to his resilience and determination. He showed the world that with hard work and perseverance, anything is possible.

Leading the Chiefs to the Super Bowl

Patrick's comeback from injury was just the beginning. He went on to lead the Chiefs to a remarkable playoff run. They defeated the Houston Texans, the Tennessee Titans, and the Baltimore Ravens to reach the Super Bowl.

"It was a dream come true," Patrick said. **"To play in the Super**

Bowl was something I had always dreamed of. It was a surreal experience."

In the Super Bowl, Patrick faced off against the San Francisco 49ers and their star quarterback, Jimmy Garoppolo. The game was a back-and-forth battle that went down to the wire.

"It was a close game," Patrick said. "We had to fight for every inch. But we never gave up. We believed in ourselves, and we were able to come out on top."

Winning MVP honors

Patrick's performance in the Super Bowl was nothing short of spectacular. He completed 26 of 42 passes for 262 yards and 2 touchdowns. He also rushed for 29 yards and a touchdown. His all-around performance helped the Chiefs defeat the 49ers by a score of 31-20.

"It was the greatest moment of my life," Patrick said. **"To win the Super Bowl with my teammates was incredible. It was a dream come true."**

For his outstanding performance in the Super Bowl, Patrick was named the game's MVP. He became the first quarterback to win Super Bowl MVP honors in his first Super Bowl appearance.

Patrick's victory in the Super Bowl cemented his status as one of the greatest quarterbacks in NFL history. He was just 24 years old, and he had already accomplished so much. The future looked bright for Patrick Mahomes, and the Chiefs were excited to see what he could do next.

CHAPTER 6:

A CHAMPION IS CROWNED

➢ **The historic Super Bowl win**

The Super Bowl was a thrilling game that went down to the wire. The Chiefs and the 49ers traded touchdowns and field goals throughout the game, and the score was tied at 20-20 with just a few minutes left to play.

Then, with the game on the line, Patrick Mahomes led the Chiefs on a dramatic drive. He completed several key passes, and Damien Williams scored the winning touchdown with just a few seconds left on the clock.

"It was the most exciting moment of my life," Patrick said. "I will never forget that feeling of

winning the Super Bowl. It was a dream come true."

The Chiefs were ecstatic. They had waited 50 years to win a Super Bowl, and they finally did it. The fans in Kansas City went wild, and the entire city was celebrating.

"It was a historic moment for our franchise," said Chiefs head coach Andy Reid. "To win the Super Bowl after all these years is incredible.

It's a moment that will be remembered forever."

Patrick Mahomes was named the Super Bowl MVP for his outstanding performance. He became the first quarterback to win Super Bowl MVP honors in his first Super Bowl appearance.

The Chiefs' victory in the Super Bowl was a moment that will be remembered for years to come. It was a historic achievement that brought joy and excitement to the entire city of Kansas City.

Mahomes' amazing performance

Patrick Mahomes' performance in the Super Bowl was nothing short of spectacular. He completed 26 of 42 passes for 262 yards and 2 touchdowns. He also rushed for 29 yards and a touchdown. His all-around performance helped the Chiefs defeat the 49ers by a score of 31-20.

"It was the greatest moment of my life," Patrick said. **"To win the Super Bowl with my teammates was incredible. It was a dream come true."**

One of the most memorable plays of the game came in the fourth quarter. With the game tied at 20-20, Patrick led the Chiefs on a crucial drive. He completed a series of passes, and Damien Williams eventually scored the winning touchdown.

"That was the biggest play of my life," Patrick said. **"I knew we had to score there. I just tried to**

stay calm and make the right plays."

Patrick's performance in the Super Bowl was a testament to his incredible talent and leadership. He was named the game's MVP, and he became the first quarterback to win Super Bowl MVP honors in his first Super Bowl appearance.

"It was a huge honor," Patrick said. "To be recognized as the best player in the game was unbelievable. It's something I'll never forget."

Becoming a football legend

Patrick Mahomes' victory in the Super Bowl cemented his status as one of the greatest quarterbacks in NFL history. He was just 24 years old, and he had already accomplished so much. The future looked bright for Patrick Mahomes, and the Chiefs were excited to see what he could do next.

"**Patrick is a once-in-a-generation talent,**" said Chiefs head coach Andy Reid. "**He's the kind of player who can change a franchise. We're so lucky to have him.**"

Patrick's victory in the Super Bowl also inspired a new generation of young football players. He showed them that with hard work, dedication, and a never-give-up attitude, anything is possible.

"I hope I can be a role model for young kids," Patrick said. "I want to show them that if you work hard and believe in yourself, you can achieve your dreams."

Patrick Mahomes' legacy is still being written. But one thing is for sure: he is already a football legend. His name will be mentioned alongside the greatest quarterbacks of all time, and his impact on the game will be felt for generations to come.

CHAPTER 7:

BEYOND THE FIELD

➤ Community involvement

Patrick Mahomes is not only a talented football player, but he is also a dedicated community leader. He is passionate about giving back to his community and making a positive difference in the world.

"I believe it's important to use my platform to make a difference," Patrick said. "I **want to inspire people to be kind, to help others, and to make the world a better place.**"

Patrick is involved in many charitable organizations. He is a supporter of the Salvation Army, the Boys & Girls Clubs of America, and the Children's Hospital of

Kansas City. He has also started his own foundation, the 15 and the Mahomies Foundation, which focuses on helping children in need.

Patrick often visits schools and hospitals to meet with children. He tells them about the importance of education, hard work, and perseverance. He also encourages them to follow their dreams and to never give up on themselves.

"I love spending time with kids," Patrick said. "They have so much energy and enthusiasm. It's inspiring to be around them."

Patrick's community involvement is an important part of his life. He believes that it is his responsibility to use his platform to make a positive impact on the world.

Philanthropic efforts

Patrick Mahomes is a generous philanthropist. He has donated millions of dollars to charitable causes, and he has been recognized for his commitment to giving back to his community.

"I believe it's important to use my blessings to help others," Patrick said. **"I'm fortunate to be in the position I'm in, and I**

want to make a difference in the world."

One of Patrick's most notable philanthropic efforts is his support of the 15 and the Mahomies Foundation. The foundation provides educational opportunities, mentorship programs, and financial assistance to children in need.

I want to give kids the opportunity to succeed, Patrick

said. **"I want to help them reach their full potential."**

Patrick has also been involved in disaster relief efforts. He has donated money and supplies to victims of hurricanes, floods, and other natural disasters.

"It's important to help people in need, no matter where they are," Patrick said. **"We're all in this together."**

Patrick's philanthropic efforts are an inspiration to others. He shows us that we can all make a difference in the world, no matter how big or small.

Inspiring the next generation

Patrick Mahomes is a role model for young people all over the world. He inspires them to follow their dreams, work hard, and never give up.

"I want to be a positive influence on young people," Patrick said. **"I want to show them that anything is possible if you believe in yourself."**

Patrick often speaks to schools and youth groups about the importance of education, hard work, and perseverance. He also encourages them to be kind, to help others, and to make a positive difference in the world.

"It's important to be a good role model," Patrick said. **"I want to show kids that it's okay to be yourself and to follow your passions."**

Patrick's impact on the next generation is immeasurable. He is a source of inspiration for young people who dream of becoming professional athletes, as well as for those who simply want to make a positive difference in the world.

"I'm grateful for the opportunity to inspire young people," Patrick said. **"It's the most rewarding thing I've ever done."**

CHAPTER 8:

THE FUTURE OF FOOTBALL

➢ Mahomes' legacy

Patrick Mahomes is already a football legend, but his story is far from over. He is still a young man, and he has many more years of football ahead of him.

"I'm just getting started," Patrick said. **"I have so much more I want to accomplish."**

Patrick's legacy as a quarterback is already secure. He is one of the most talented and exciting players of his generation. He has won a Super Bowl, been named the NFL MVP, and broken numerous records.

"Patrick is a generational talent," said Chiefs head coach Andy Reid. **"He's the kind of**

player who comes along once in a lifetime."

But Patrick's impact on the game goes beyond his individual achievements. He has changed the way the quarterback position is played. He is known for his ability to make plays off-script, his incredible arm strength, and his fearless style of play.

"Patrick has revolutionized the quarterback position," said former NFL quarterback Brett Favre.

"He's a game-changer."

As Patrick continues to play, his legacy will only grow. He will continue to inspire young football players, and he will continue to entertain fans with his incredible talent.

"I want to be remembered as a great player and a good person," Patrick said. **"I want to**

leave a positive impact on the game and on the world."

The future of football is bright, and Patrick Mahomes is at the forefront of it. He is a true superstar, and his story is far from over.

Continuing to break records

Patrick Mahomes is a record-breaking machine. He has already broken numerous NFL records, and there is no doubt that he will continue to add to his impressive resume.

"I love breaking records," Patrick said. **"It's a challenge, and it's**

something that I'm always striving for."

One of Patrick's biggest goals is to break Tom Brady's record for most Super Bowl championships. Brady has won seven Super Bowls, and Patrick is determined to catch him.

"Tom Brady is a legend," Patrick said. **"He's the greatest quarterback of all time. But I'm going to try to catch him."**

In addition to breaking records, Patrick also wants to continue to be a leader for the Chiefs. He wants to help the team win multiple Super Bowls and establish themselves as one of the most dominant franchises in the NFL.

"I want to build a dynasty here in Kansas City," Patrick said. **"I want to win multiple Super Bowls and leave a lasting legacy."**

The future looks bright for Patrick Mahomes and the Kansas City Chiefs. With Patrick at the helm, the Chiefs are a force to be reckoned with. They are a team that is capable of winning multiple Super Bowls and establishing themselves as one of the greatest dynasties in NFL history.

Inspiring young athletes

Patrick Mahomes is a role model for young athletes all over the world. He inspires them to follow their dreams, work hard, and never give up.

"I want to be a positive influence on young people," Patrick said. **"I want to show**

them that anything is possible if you believe in yourself."

Patrick often speaks to schools and youth groups about the importance of education, hard work, and perseverance. He also encourages them to be kind, to help others, and to make a positive difference in the world.

"It's important to be a good role model," Patrick said. **"I want to show kids that it's okay to be**

yourself and to follow your passions."

Patrick's impact on the next generation is immeasurable. He is a source of inspiration for young people who dream of becoming professional athletes, as well as for those who simply want to make a positive difference in the world.

"I'm grateful for the opportunity to inspire young people," Patrick said. **"It's the**

most rewarding thing I've ever done."

Patrick Mahomes is a true superstar, and his story is far from over. He is a role model for young athletes everywhere, and he is sure to continue to inspire people for years to come.

PATRICK MAHOMES FUN FACTS

1. **He's a Baseball Star's Son:** Patrick's dad, Pat Mahomes, was a Major League Baseball pitcher.

2. **He's Left-Handed:** While many quarterbacks are right-handed, Patrick is a lefty.

3. **He's a Pizza Lover:** Patrick loves pizza and is often seen eating it after games.

4. **He's a Dog Dad:** Patrick has a dog named Stilton, who is often seen with him at games and events.

5. **He's a Philanthropist:** Patrick is involved in many charitable organizations and is a strong supporter of community initiatives.

6. **He's a Super Bowl Champion:** Patrick led the Kansas City Chiefs to their first Super Bowl victory in 50 years in 2020.

7. **He's a Record-Breaker:** Patrick has broken numerous NFL records, including the single-season passing yards record.

8. **He's a Fashion Icon:** Patrick is known for his stylish outfits

and has been featured in several fashion magazines.

9. **He's a Gamer:** Patrick enjoys playing video games in his free time.

10. **He's a Family Man:** Patrick is married and has a daughter.

PATRICK MAHOMES

QUOTES

1. "Never give up on your dreams."

2. "Hard work pays off."

3. "Believe in yourself."

4. "It's okay to make mistakes."

5. "Always strive for greatness."

6. "Be kind to others."

7. "Follow your passion."

8. "Never stop learning."

9. "Teamwork makes the dream work."

10. "It's important to have fun."

PATRICK MAHOMES

TIMELINE

Early Life (1995-2014)

1. **1995:** Born in Tyler, Texas.

2. **2003:** Begins playing baseball and football.

3. **2014:** Commits to Texas Tech University.

College Career (2015-2017)

1. **2015:** Freshman season at Texas Tech.
2. **2016:** Sophomore season, sets numerous records.
3. **2017:** Junior season, Heisman Trophy finalist.

NFL Career (2017-present)

1. **2017:** Drafted first overall by the Kansas City Chiefs.

2. **2018:** NFL Offensive Rookie of the Year.

3. **2019:** Leads the Chiefs to the Super Bowl and wins MVP.

4. **2020:** Wins Super Bowl MVP.

5. **2021:** Signs a 10-year contract extension with the Chiefs.

6. **2023:** Continues to break records and lead the Chiefs to playoff appearances.

Key Achievements

1. Super Bowl champion (2020)

2. Super Bowl MVP (2020)

3. NFL MVP (2020)

4. NFL Offensive Player of the Year (2018)

5. NFL Offensive Rookie of the Year (2018)

6. 4x Pro Bowl selection

7. 2x First-team All-Pro

8. Big 12 Offensive Player of the Year (2016, 2017)

9. Heisman Trophy finalist (2017)

10. Numerous NFL records

FOOTBALL TERMS FOR KIDS

Basic Terms

1. **Football:** The ball used in the game.

2. **Field:** The playing area.

3. **End Zone:** The area at each end of the field where touchdowns are scored.

4. **Touchdown:** A score worth 6 points.

5. **Extra Point:** A kick worth 1 point after a touchdown.

6. **Field Goal:** A kick worth 3 points.

7. **Fumble:** Losing possession of the ball.

8. **Interception:** Catching a pass intended for the other team.

9. **Sack:** Tackling the quarterback behind the line of scrimmage.

10. **Penalty:** A rule violation that results in a loss of yards.

Positions

1. **Quarterback (QB):** The player who throws the ball.

2. **Running Back (RB):** The player who carries the ball.

3. **Wide Receiver (WR):** The player who catches passes.

4. **Tight End (TE):** A player who can block or catch passes.

5. **Offensive Line:** The players who protect the quarterback and create running lanes.

6. **Defensive Line:** The players who try to stop the offense.

7. **Linebacker (LB):** The players who play between the defensive line and the secondary.

8. **Secondary:** The players who cover receivers and try to intercept passes.

Plays

1. **Pass:** Throwing the ball to a receiver.

2. **Run:** Carrying the ball.

3. **Screen Pass:** A pass to a running back who is protected by the offensive line.

4. **Blitz:** An aggressive defensive play where multiple players rush the quarterback.

5. **Coverage:** The defensive strategy for defending passes.

Rules

1. **Down:** A series of plays that starts after the ball is snapped.

2. **First Down:** Gaining 10 yards or more on a play.

3. **Fourth Down:** The fourth and final play in a series. If the offense doesn't get a first down, they lose possession of the ball.

4. **Turnover:** When the offense loses possession of the ball to the defense.

PATRICK MAHOMES QUIZ

1. What sport did Patrick Mahomes play before he started playing football?

- A. Basketball

- B. Baseball

- C. Soccer

2. What college did Patrick Mahomes attend?

- A. Texas

- B. Texas A&M

- C. Texas Tech

3. What position does Patrick Mahomes play in the NFL?

- A. Wide Receiver
- B. Running Back
- C. Quarterback

4. What team does Patrick Mahomes play for in the NFL?

- A. Kansas City Chiefs
- B. New England Patriots
- C. Green Bay Packers

5. **What** **year** **did** **Patrick** **Mahomes win the Super Bowl?**

- A. 2020

- B. 2021

- C. 2022

6. What is the name of Patrick Mahomes' dog?

- A. Stilton

- B. Cooper

- C. Riley

7. What is Patrick Mahomes' favorite food?

- A. Pizza

- B. Tacos

- C. Steak

8. What is Patrick Mahomes' jersey number?

- A. 10

- B. 12

- C. 15

9. What award did Patrick Mahomes win in his rookie year?

- A. Offensive Rookie of the Year
- B. Defensive Rookie of the Year
- C. Rookie of the Year

10. What is the name of Patrick Mahomes' foundation?

- A. The 15 and the Mahomies Foundation
- B. The Mahomes Foundation

- C. The Mahomes Family Foundation

Made in the USA
Monee, IL
30 November 2024

71659703R00066